Spider Magic

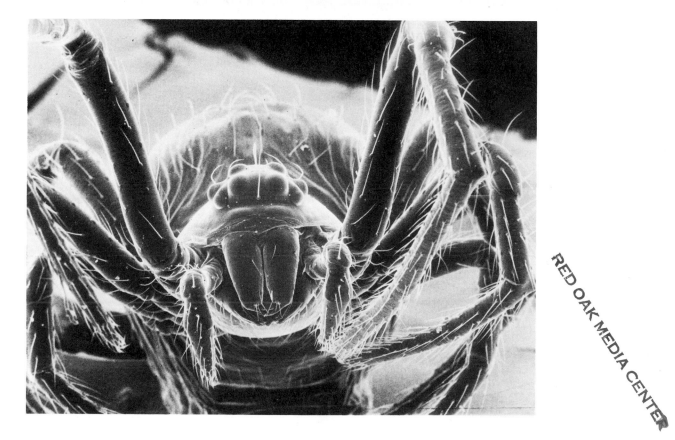

Dorothy Hinshaw Patent

Holiday House
NEW YORK

To Diane Bilderback, *who appreciates spiders*

Library of Congress Cataloging in Publication Data

Patent, Dorothy Hinshaw.
  Spider magic.

  Includes index.
  Summary: Describes the characteristics, behavior, and
special organs of different spiders including the water
spider, orb web spider, black widow, and tarantula.
    1. Spiders—Juvenile literature.   [1. Spiders]
I. Title.
QL458.4.P38   595.4′4   81-85088
ISBN 0-8234-0438-2   AACR2

TITLE PAGE PHOTOGRAPH:
DR. J. NORMAN GRIM,
NORTHERN ARIZONA UNIVERSITY

Contents

What Are Spiders?

Everyone knows what spiders look like. They live in our houses. They live in our gardens and parks. Many people think that spiders are insects. They look like insects in some ways, but they are not insects.

This spider from New Zealand makes a web that looks like a funnel. RAINER FOELIX

Insects have six legs. Spiders have eight legs. Insects have three parts to their bodies—a head, a thorax (THOR-aks), and an abdomen (AB-doh-men). Spiders have only two body parts. Like insects, they have an abdomen. But their head and thorax are combined into one section called the cephalothorax (SEF-ah-lo-THOR-aks).

head

thorax

abdomen

Here is an ant attacking a worm. You can see the three parts of the ant's body and its antennae, its big eyes, and its six legs.
STEPHEN DALTON © 1973

6

Here is a poisonous brown recluse spider biting a cricket. The spider has eight legs and two body parts. It has no antennae. You can see its pedipalps holding the cricket. If you look closely, you can see its jaws biting the cricket. Its eyes are too small to see clearly.
RAINER FOELIX

abdomen

cephalothorax

pedipalps

jaws

Most insects have two big eyes, one on each side of the head. Many insects also have three small eyes between the big ones. But spiders generally have eight eyes. Insects have antennae on their heads. Spiders do not. But spiders do have a pair of "pedipalps" (PED-ee-pahlps) that look like short extra front legs. They also have a pair of very strong jaws with pointed fangs for capturing their food.

Many people do not like spiders. They are afraid of them. But most spiders will not hurt people. They are usually helpful, since they catch and eat harmful insects.

7

How Spiders Sense the World

The eyes of most spiders are very small. They do not see very much. But spiders have other ways of knowing what is going on around them. They have many hairs on their legs and bodies which sense touch. They also have tiny slits supplied with nerves which probably feel movements of their webs.

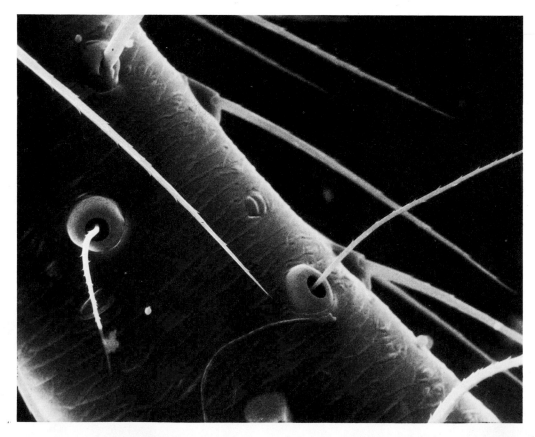

These tiny hairs on a spider's leg help it to sense touch. They've been blown up in the photograph to 1,600 times their normal size.

DR. J. NORMAN GRIM,
NORTHERN ARIZONA UNIVERSITY

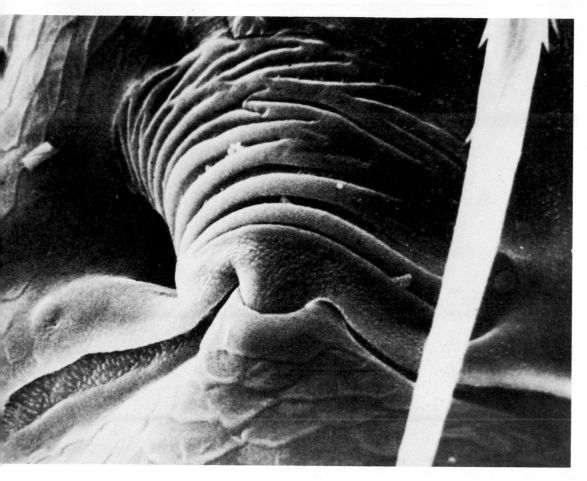

See the tiny slits? They're on the spider's leg, and have also been blown up to many times their normal size. These slits probably sense movements of the web. RAINER FOELIX

Spiders do not taste with their mouths like humans do. They use their feet instead. Their feet also sense water. If the front foot of a thirsty spider touches water, the spider steps forward to drink. If a hind foot touches water, the spider turns around and drinks.

How Spiders Use Silk

All spiders depend on silk. Underneath or at the rear end of the abdomen, every spider has a set of silk spinners. These are called spinnerets. If you could see them blown up, they'd look like nozzles covered with tiny holes. Very thin strands of silk come through the holes. They combine to make the silken lines that you can see. Some of the spinnerets make silk for webs. Others make silk for sacs which protect the spider's eggs.

silk →

The black widow spider has her spinnerets at the rear of her body. She is letting out a line of silk from her spinnerets.
RAINER FOELIX

10

All spiders have spinnerets for making a strong double strand of silk called the dragline. The spider spins the dragline as it walks along. Every now and then the spider stops to glue it down. The dragline allows the spider to find its way back to where it was. The dragline also holds the spider when it jumps off a high place to escape an enemy.

Many spiders make webs. The most familiar is the orb web, which looks like a wagon wheel. Some webs are tangled masses of threads. Others are sheets made from many strands of silk laid closely together.

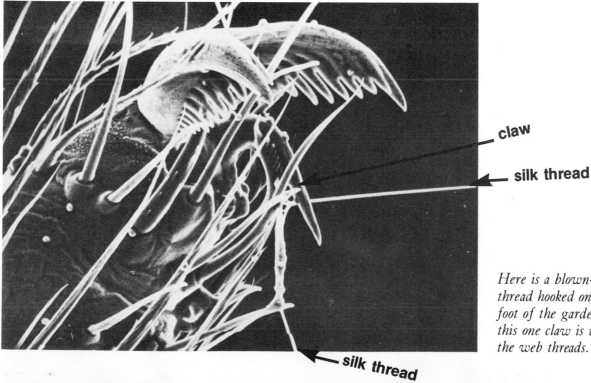

claw

silk thread

silk thread

Here is a blown-up photo of silk thread hooked onto a claw on the foot of the garden spider. Only this one claw is used to grab the web threads. RAINER FOELIX

11

How Spiders Eat

Spiders have very small mouths. They have strong jaws but no teeth. They do not take bites of food and swallow them. When a spider captures an insect, it injects poison through its hollow fangs into the insect's body. The poison causes the insect to stop struggling. The spider also injects chemicals which digest the insect's insides, turning them to liquid. Then the spider sucks up the fluid.

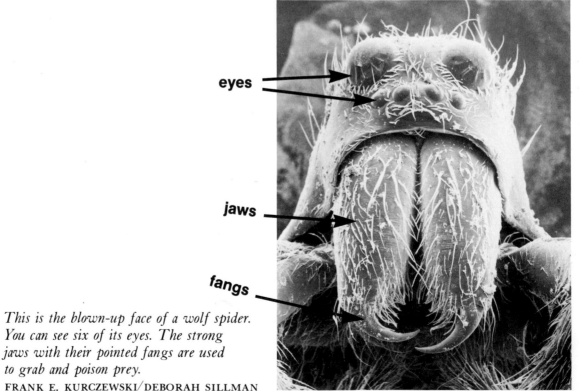

eyes

jaws

fangs

This is the blown-up face of a wolf spider. You can see six of its eyes. The strong jaws with their pointed fangs are used to grab and poison prey.
FRANK E. KURCZEWSKI/DEBORAH SILLMAN

Not all spiders eat only insects. Some feed on other spiders. A few spiders are big enough to eat small birds or lizards, too. A few spiders even eat fish.

Some spiders, like this big-eyed jumping spider, eat other spiders.
E. S. ROSS

Spider Families

Most spiders have very little family life. The male and female come together only to mate. The male spider then goes away and often dies. The female spider spins a special egg sac to protect her eggs. Some spiders leave the egg sac in a protected place and go away. But others take care of it. The female black widow spider hangs her egg sac in her web during the day. She brings it into her shelter with her at night. Many hunting spiders carry their egg sacs around with them. Certain baby spiders stay with the mother for awhile after they hatch.

With some kinds of spiders, all the babies from one egg sac stay together after hatching. They spin a tiny web. If they are startled, they cluster together on the web. When they are not disturbed, they spread out. After a few days, each little spider climbs up to a high spot. It lets out a strand of silk. The wind catches the silk, and the baby spider flies off to make a new home for itself.

Male spiders are usually smaller than females. These two house spiders (the male is on the right) are about to mate.
RAINER FOELIX

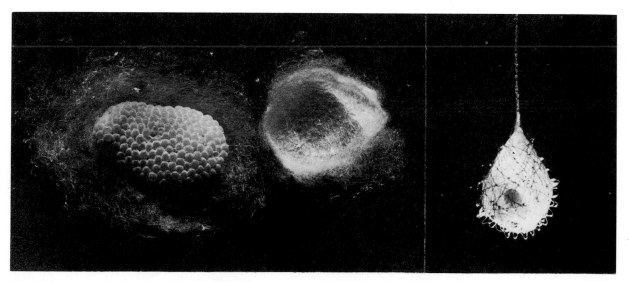

Female spiders make special sacs for their eggs. On the left is an opened garden spider sac. The sac on the right belongs to a pirate spider. RAINER FOELIX

15

Here is the empty old skeleton of a tarantula. Even the smallest hairs are shed along with the skeleton. RAINER FOELIX

A garden spider pulls itself upside down out of its old skeleton. You can see its eyes as dark spots at the bottom of the picture. RAINER FOELIX

How Spiders Grow

Spiders have a hard outer covering on their bodies. This covering helps protect them from enemies and from the dry air. It acts as a skeleton, too. Because their hard skeleton is on the outside, spiders cannot grow bit by bit the way people do. The hard covering will not stretch. When spiders grow, they must shed the entire skeleton first. They do all their growing before the new skeleton hardens. The old skeleton splits down the back, and the spider pulls itself out carefully. Getting its long legs safely out can be tricky. The spider begins to grow as the legs are being pulled out. It finishes growing within minutes or hours. When it first comes out, the spider is weak. Its muscles have no hard skeleton to pull against. But in a short while, its new skeleton hardens. Most spiders shed their skeletons and grow like this seven to ten times before they are full grown.

Orb Web Spiders

Orb web spiders are very common. They often live in gardens. Their webs are beautiful, especially when covered by the morning dew. To build its web, the orb weaver starts by making a strong top thread which stretches across an opening. Then it makes the spokes of the web and the outside threads which hold the web together. Next, the spider makes a wide spiral which holds the spokes together. Finally, it replaces the wide spiral with a new spiral of sticky threads. When an insect hits the threads, it gets stuck. The spider can grab it and bite it before it can escape.

Many different spiders build orb webs. Some orb weavers are large and some are small. Some are plain and some are colorful. But all have an especially good trap for catching insects.

You can see the small eyes of this orb-weaving garden spider. It is waiting at the center of its web.
The thick zigzag threads probably strengthen the web.
RAINER FOELIX

18

The orb web is very beautiful.
You can trace the sticky spiral
from the outside all the way to
the center of the web.
JEANNE WHITE FROM
NATIONAL AUDUBON SOCIETY

19

Crab Spiders

Crab spiders do not build webs. They lay in wait, often on flowers, for their prey. Many crab spiders can change color from white to yellow and back again. They wait on flowers of the same color, so they are hard to see. Crab spiders feed on bees and other insects which visit flowers. Their front legs are long. They are turned forwards so the spider can grab its food fast. Crab spiders have very poisonous venom that acts quickly. This protects them from the sting of bees, which are their most common food.

A crab spider hides among the flowers, waiting for insects.
RAINER FOELIX

20

*This yellow crab spider on a yellow flower
has caught a honeybee.* BILL MUNOZ

Jumping Spiders

Jumping spiders do not make webs either. Jumping spiders are easy to recognize. They are usually small and chunky with rather short legs. They move in quick jerky steps and sudden leaps. They have a pair of very big front eyes and six smaller eyes. Using its big eyes, a jumping spider can see clearly a foot away.

Jumping spiders often live in or around houses. They can be seen on windows, stalking ants or flies. They have clumps of special tiny sticky claws on their feet which make it easy for them to climb glass.

Some male jumping spiders are brightly colored. They may have bands of color on their front legs. They attract females by waving their legs and dancing about.

The jumping spider has big front eyes for spotting its prey. TROYER AND FOELIX

Wolf Spiders

Wolf spiders are hunters, too. They look different from jumping spiders. Their bodies are slimmer. Their legs are longer. They run along smoothly and do not jump suddenly. Wolf spiders are often light brown or gray and have a fine coat of short hairs on their bodies. Wolf spiders have one large pair of eyes above a row of four small eyes. They also have another pair of eyes on top of the head which look upward.

Wolf spiders have long legs and powerful jaws. You can see four of their eyes in this photograph.
RAINER FOELIX

23

Female wolf spiders carry their egg sacs around with them. After the young spiders hatch, they climb onto their mothers' abdomen. They stay with her for a week or so before going out on their own.

The female wolf spider carries her babies around for several days after they hatch. E. S. ROSS

The Cellar Spider

The cellar spider lives in houses. It is found in almost every country. The pale whitish cellar spider is only about ¼-inch long, but its legs are 2 inches long. Cellar spiders make tangled webs, often in corners. When the webs become dusty, people call them "cobwebs."

The cellar spider's web is not sticky. When an insect hits the web, the spider shakes the web with its legs. This helps tangle the struggling insect so it cannot get away.

The female cellar spider carries her delicate egg sac around in her jaws. When the baby spiders hatch, she hangs the sac in the web and guards them as they come out.

The cellar spider has very long legs. The female here is carrying her egg sac in her jaws. RAINER FOELIX

The Black Widow

The black widow is a beautiful, shiny spider. But she is dangerous. Her bite can make a person very sick. Some people have died from black widow bites. No other spider looks quite like the black widow. Her shiny black body has a large abdomen and long thin legs. She usually has a red marking on the underside of her abdomen. This marking is usually shaped like an hourglass, but not always. If you see a shiny black spider, stay away from it. It could be a black widow, even if it does not have the hourglass marking.

Black widows often live in woodpiles or rock gardens. They sometimes live in basements, too. The black widow web is made of tangled threads. The spider mostly hides near the web, waiting for insects to become trapped.

The male black widow does not have a poisonous bite. He is smaller than the female and has brown striped legs.

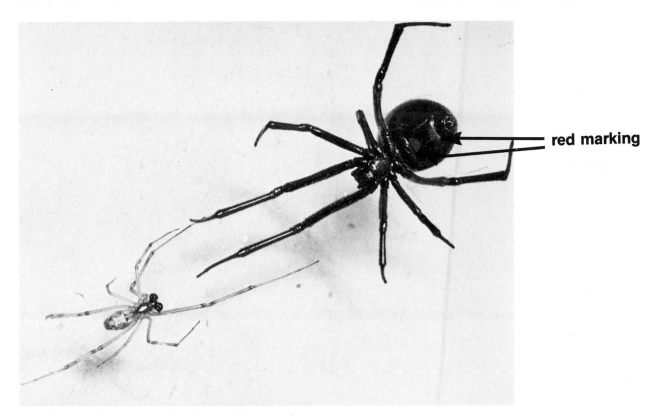

red marking

The female black widow (on the right) is much larger and darker than her harmless mate. The red marking on this female is incomplete. It looks like two triangles instead of an hourglass. KENNETH ROSS

This black widow from South America has pretty red-and-white markings on her abdomen.
RAINER FOELIX

27

Tarantulas

Tarantulas are big, hairy spiders. Many people are afraid of them. But the tarantulas that live in the United States are not poisonous to people. They are actually very gentle and made good pets. Our tarantulas live mostly in the southwestern deserts.

Tropical tarantulas often live in damp places. Many of them spend their lives in the trees. Some are poisonous to humans. The largest tarantulas live in South American jungles. Their legs may span 10 inches, and they can feed on birds. Some can even kill and feed on small poisonous snakes.

Tarantulas are big, strong, hairy spiders.
RAINER FOELIX

Trapdoor Spiders

Many spiders build sheltered silk tunnels to rest in. But the trapdoor spider stays in its home almost all the time. It builds a door to its tunnel. The door has a hinge. The spider can close and open the door. When the weather is bad or the spider is resting, the door is closed. But when the spider is hungry, it waits at the top of its tunnel. It holds the door open just a bit. When an insect passes near, the spider quickly rushes out just far enough to grab the insect. Then it dashes back into its home with its dinner.

Male trapdoor spiders leave their homes to find mates. The females lay their eggs in their tunnels. The little spiderlings stay in their mother's tunnel for a few weeks after hatching. The tunnel protects them from hungry enemies.

The trapdoor spider lives in a silken tunnel with a hinged door covering the opening.
FREDERICK A. COYLE

*This trapdoor spider has pushed open the door
to its silken tunnel so it can come out.*

© LYNWOOD M. CHACE FROM NATIONAL AUDUBON SOCIETY

31

The Fisher Spider

The fisher spider is a big, strong hunter. It looks like a very large wolf spider. The biggest American fisher spider has a body 1½ inches long. The fisher spider lives near lakes and streams. It eats water insects and insects which get caught on the water's surface. It can run on top of the water to capture these insects. It can even dive under the water to catch small fish. When it dives, a thin film of air is trapped by its body hairs. This helps the spider breathe underwater.

The female fisher spider carries her egg sac until the baby spiders are ready to hatch. Then she hangs it on a plant. She pulls down some leaves to protect it. She spins some silk to hold the leaves together. This makes a cozy nursery for the young spiders. The mother spider stays near. She guards her babies for about a week until they shed their skeletons the first time. Then they leave the nursery, and she stops guarding it.

The fisher spider is a powerful hunter.
This one has caught a cricket.
RAINER FOELIX

The Water Spider

The fisher spider spends most of its time out of the water. But the European water spider lives its whole life under water. It spins a thick silk sheet and attaches it to water plants. Then it makes many trips to the surface and collects small bubbles, one at a time. It puts them under the silk sheet, making one big bubble. This is the spider's home.

The water spider spends most of its time there. It leaves the bubble to hunt at night, catching water insects. It brings the food back to its bubble nest for eating. At mating time, the male water spider builds his bubble next to the female's. Then he makes a silk tube to connect them. The female water spider hangs her egg sac in her bubble. When the baby spiders hatch, they stay in their mother's bubble for awhile. Soon they leave and make their own bubble homes.

*This water spider has caught an insect larva and
is carrying it to the bubble nest to eat it.*
FRITZ VOLLRATH

Spiders That Look Like Ants

Many spiders look like ants. Ants are not eaten by most animals. They often taste bad. They have stinging sprays to protect themselves. A spider which looks like an ant probably is protected from being eaten.

An ant looks very different from a normal spider. It has three body parts. The spider has only two. It has antennae. The spider has none. An ant's legs are shorter than a spider's legs.

Ant spiders have different ways of looking ant-like. Some have dark markings on the front part of the body. These markings make it look as if the spider has three body parts. Many ant spiders hold up their front legs and wave them about. Then they look like antennae instead of legs. Ant spiders even move like ants. They run with short nervous steps the way ants do.

*This spider lives in Thailand. It looks
very much like a* Polyrachis *ant.*
E. S. ROSS

37

Social Spiders

Most spiders stay away from other spiders. But a few kinds live together in large numbers. They work together to build huge webs. The webs of social spiders may completely cover bushes or small trees. Alone, one of these small spiders could not capture big insects. But by helping each other, they can catch and eat insects much larger than themselves.

Many Kinds of Spiders

In this book you have learned about some spiders. There are many other sorts of spiders, too. Some live on high mountains. Others make their homes in hot deserts. Over 30,000 kinds of spiders are known. But some people think that there are 120,000 still to be discovered. Even scientists still have a lot to learn about spiders.

Social spiders share a large web. Here (left) a female spider gives a baby food from her own mouth. On the right, other young spiders feed together on a fly.
RAINER FOELIX

Index